glee The 3D Concert Movie

MOTION PICTURE SOUNDTRACK

GUITAR

Series Artwork, Fox Trademarks and Logos
TM and © 2011 Twentieth Century Fox Film Corporation.
All Rights Reserved.

ISBN 978-1-4584-1722-0

HAL•LEONARD®
CORPORATION

7777 W. BLUEMOUND RD. P.O. BOX 13819 MILWAUKEE, WI 53213

Visit Hal Leonard Online at
www.halleonard.com

DON'T STOP BELIEVIN'

Words and Music by STEVE PERRY,
NEAL SCHON and JONATHAN CAIN

Male: Just a small-town girl, _____
Female: Just a city boy, _____

DOG DAYS ARE OVER

Words and Music by FLORENCE WELCH
and ISABELLA SUMMERS

Indie Rock

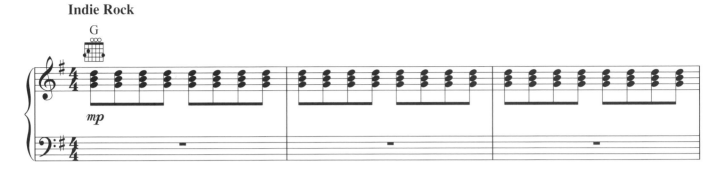

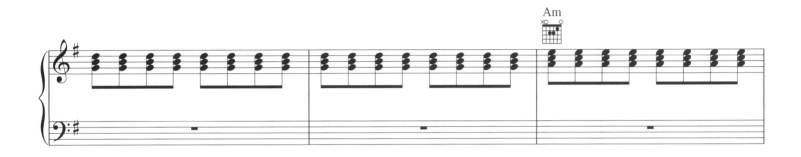

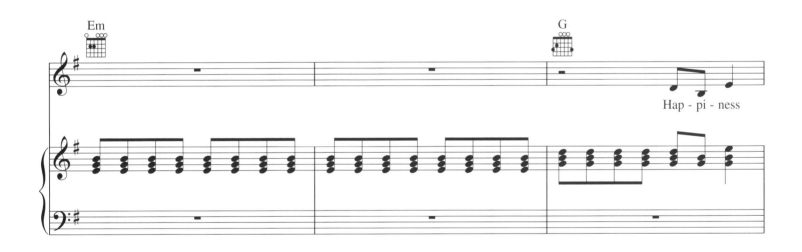

Hap - pi - ness

hit her   like a train____ on __ a track.___

SING

Words and Music by FRANK IERO,
RAY TORO, MIKEY WAY
and GERARD WAY

I'M A SLAVE 4 U

Words and Music by PHARRELL WILLIAMS
and CHAD HUGO

Dance Pop

All you peo-ple look at me like I'm a lit-tle girl. Well, did you

ev-er think it be o-kay for me to step in-to this world?

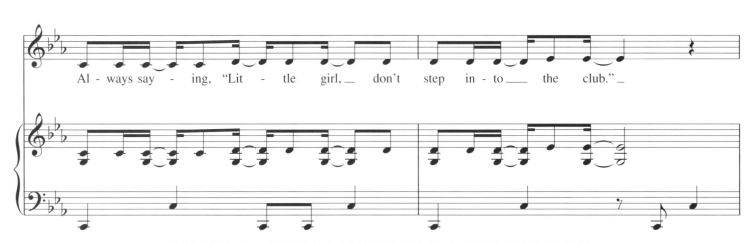

Al-ways say-ing, "Lit-tle girl, don't step in-to the club."

28

D.S. al Coda

I'm not try'n' to hide _ it. *(1st time only)* Like that.

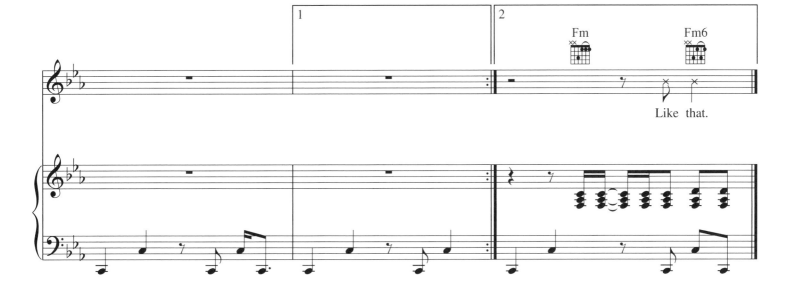

Like that.

FAT BOTTOMED GIRLS

Words and Music by
BRIAN MAY

Are you gon - na take me home to - night?

Ah, down be - side that red fire - light.

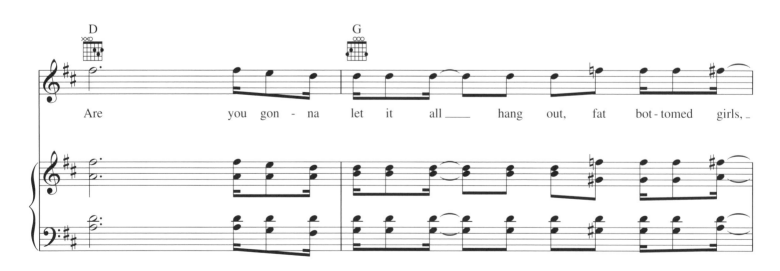

Are you gon - na let it all hang out, fat bot - tomed girls,

I WANT TO HOLD YOUR HAND

Words and Music by JOHN LENNON
and PAUL McCARTNEY

Gentle Folk

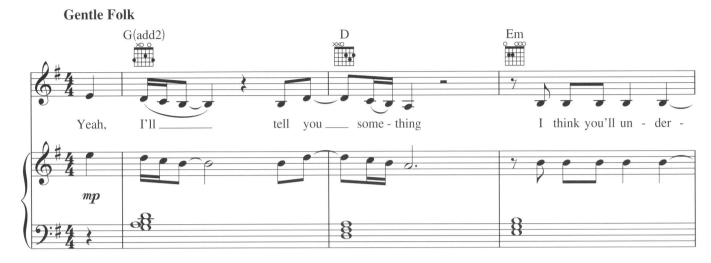

Yeah, I'll _____ tell you _____ some-thing I think you'll un-der-

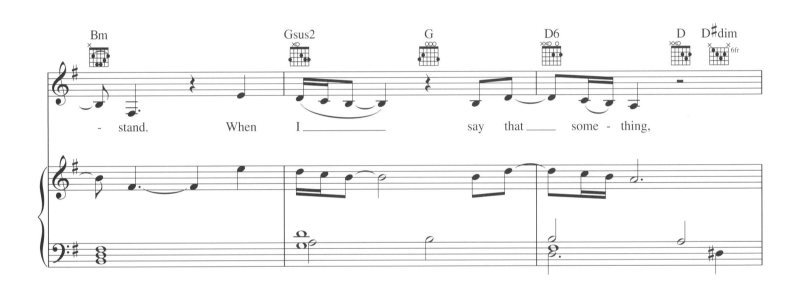

-stand. When I _____ say that _____ some-thing,

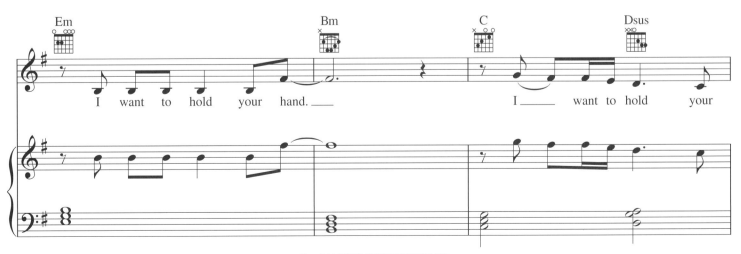

I want to hold your hand. _____ I _____ want to hold your

AIN'T NO WAY

Words and Music by
CAROLYN FRANKLIN

P.Y.T.
(Pretty Young Thing)

Words and Music by QUINCY JONES
and JAMES INGRAM

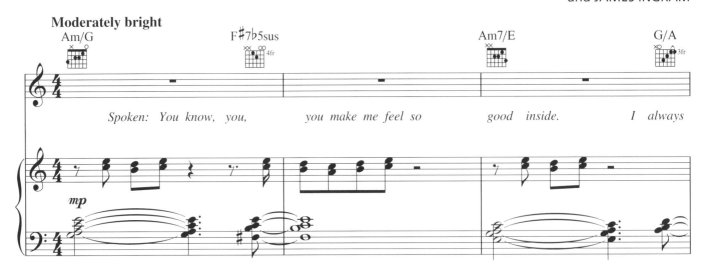

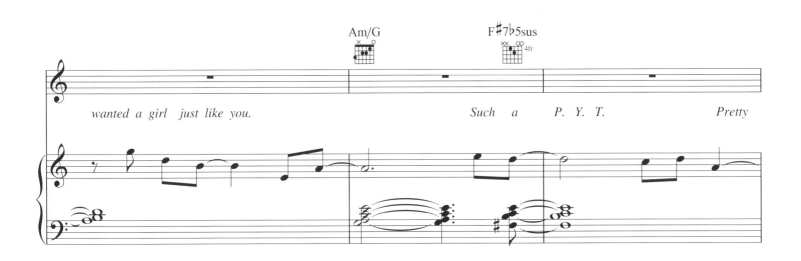

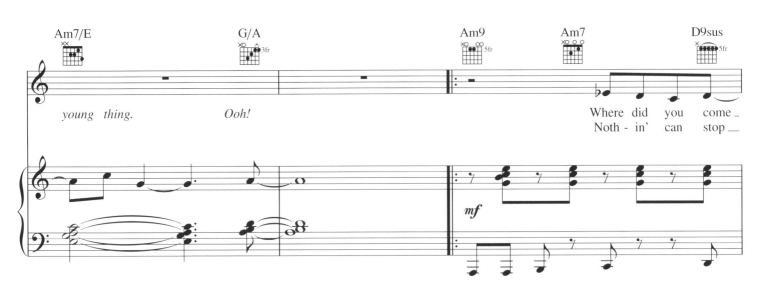

BORN THIS WAY

Words and Music by STEFANI GERMANOTTA,
JEPPE LAURSEN, FERNANDO GARIBAY
and PAUL BLAIR

* *Recorded a half step lower.*

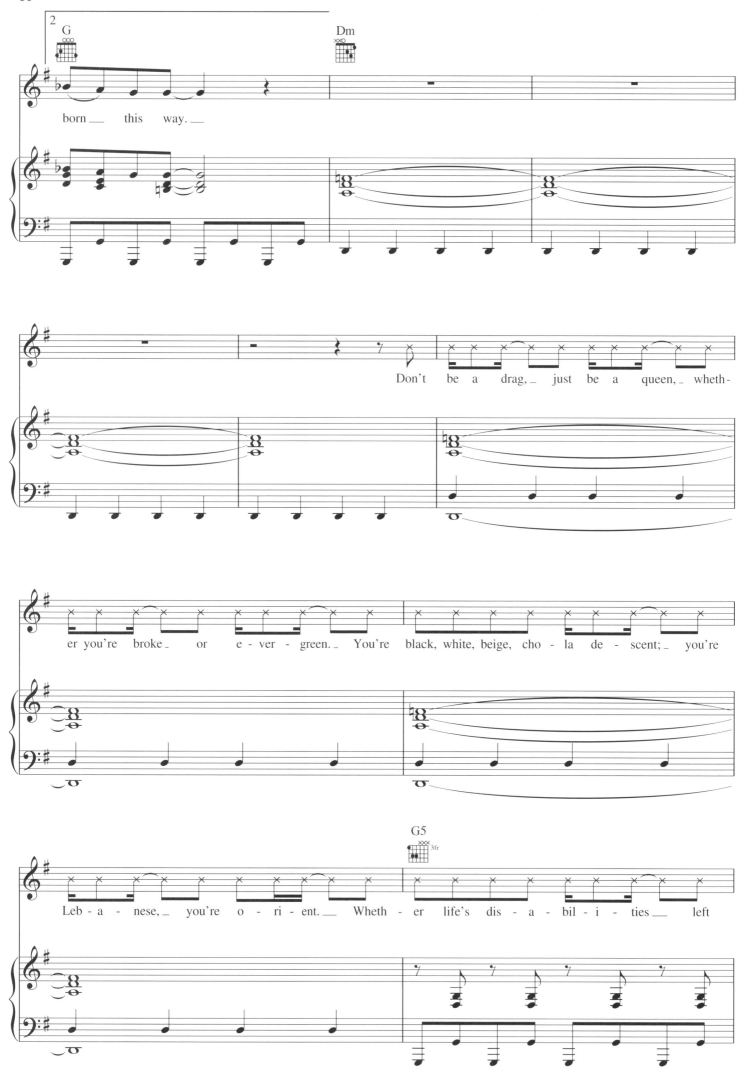

58

FIREWORK

Words and Music by MIKKEL ERIKSEN,
TOR ERIK HERMANSEN, ESTHER DEAN,
KATY PERRY and SANDY WILHELM

TEENAGE DREAM

Words and Music by LUKASZ GOTTWALD,
MAX MARTIN, BENJAMIN LEVIN,
BONNIE McKEE and KATY PERRY

69

SILLY LOVE SONGS

Words and Music by PAUL McCARTNEY
and LINDA McCARTNEY

RAISE YOUR GLASS

Words and Music by ALECIA MOORE,
MAX MARTIN and JOHAN SCHUSTER

HAPPY DAYS ARE HERE AGAIN/ GET HAPPY

HAPPY DAYS ARE HERE AGAIN
Words by JACK YELLEN
Music by MILTON AGER

GET HAPPY
from SUMMER STOCK
Lyric by TED KOEHLER
Music by HAROLD ARLEN

head - ing _____ 'cross the riv - er, _____ soon your cares will all be gone.

There'll

be no _____ more _____ from now _____ on, _____ from now

For - get your trou - bles _____ and just get hap -

on. Hap - py days

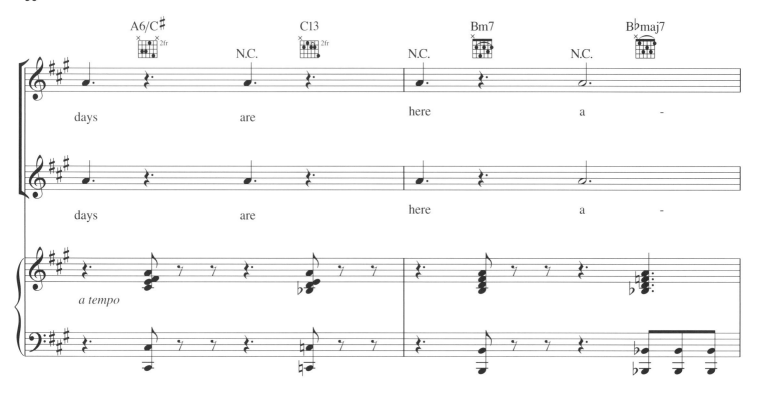

days   are   here   a -

days   are   here   a -

a tempo

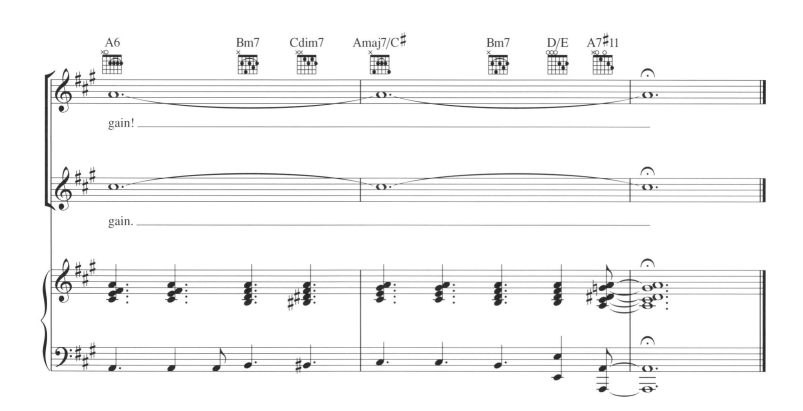

gain! _____

gain. _____

Lucky

Words and Music by JASON MRAZ,
COLBIE CAILLAT and TIMOTHY FAGAN

D.S. al Coda

RIVER DEEP - MOUNTAIN HIGH

Words and Music by JEFF BARRY,
ELLIE GREENWICH and PHIL SPECTOR

98

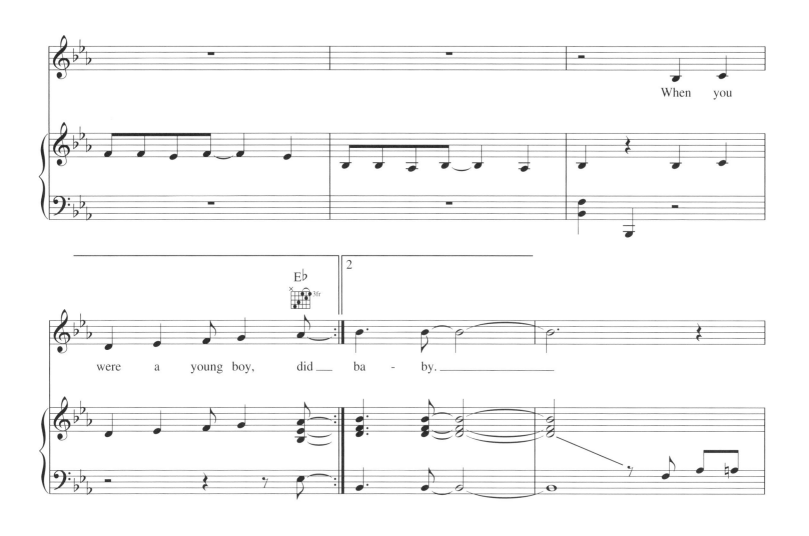

When you were a young boy, did ___ ba - by. ___

I love you, ba - by like ___ a flow-

- er loves __ the spring; __ and I love you, ba-

- by, like __ the rob - in loves __ to sing. __

I love you, ba - by, like __ a school - boy loves his

pie; and I love you, ba - by, riv - er deep

FORGET YOU

Words and Music by BRUNO MARS,
ARI LEVINE, PHILIP LAWRENCE,
THOMAS CALLAWAY and BRODY BROWN

DON'T RAIN ON MY PARADE

Words by BOB MERRILL
Music by JULE STYNE

JESSIE'S GIRL

Words and Music by
RICK SPRINGFIELD

120

VALERIE

Words and Music by SEAN PAYNE,
DAVID McCABE, ABIGAIL HARDING,
BOYAN CHOWDHURY and RUSSELL PRITCHARD

Up-beat Soul

Well, some - times I go out —

— by my - self — and I — look a - cross — the wa -

LOSER LIKE ME

Words and Music by ADAM ANDERS,
PEER ASTROM, MAX MARTIN,
SAVAN KOTECHA and JOHAN SCHUSTER

keep the "L" ___ up, 'cause I don't care. You can throw your sticks and you can throw your stones,

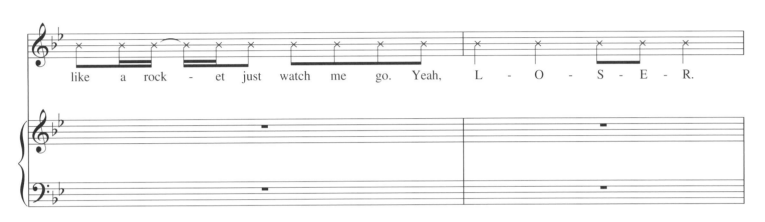

like a rock - et just watch me go. Yeah, L - O - S - E - R.

I can on - ly be who I are. Just go a - head ___ and hate on me and run your mouth ___

___ so ev - 'ry - one can hear. Hit me with ___ the worst you've got and knock me down. ___

THE SAFETY DANCE

Words and Music by
IVAN DOROSCHUK

We can dance if we want to, we can leave your friends be - hind. ___ 'Cause your

friends don't dance, and if ___ they don't dance, well, they're no friends of mine. ___ Say, ___

144

Yes, safe - ty dance. ___

To next strain   Fine

D.S. al Fine

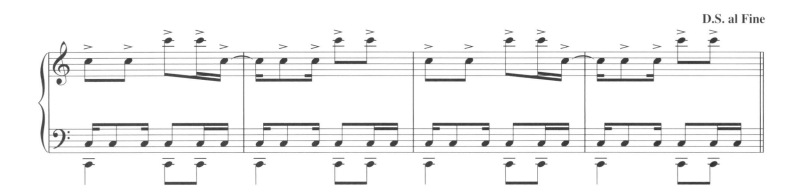

SOMEBODY TO LOVE

Words and Music by
FREDDIE MERCURY

find me some-bod-y to love, ____ find me some-bod-y to love, ____

find me some-bod-y to love. _____

Find me some-bod-y to love, ____ find me some-bod-y to love, ____

Eb/Ab Db/Ab Ab

some-bod-y, some-bod-y, some-bod-y some-bod-y, some-bod-y. Find me some-bod-y, find me some

155

glee-full collections!
Get hip with music featured on the blockbuster TV show.

  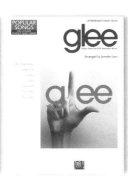 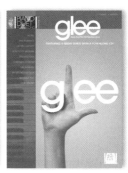  

Piano/Vocal/Guitar

Glee
00313479 P/V/G..........................$16.99

More Songs from Glee
00313491 P/V/G..........................$16.99

Glee – The Christmas Album
00313566 P/V/G..........................$16.99

Glee – The Showstoppers
00313512 P/V/G..........................$16.99

Glee – Journey to Regionals
00313516 P/V/G..........................$12.99

Glee – The Power of Madonna
00313507 P/V/G..........................$14.99

Glee – The Rocky Horror Glee Show
00313528 P/V/G..........................$12.99

Glee – The Warblers
00313567 P/V/G..........................$16.99

Glee – Season Two, Volume 4
00313533 P/V/G..........................$16.99

Glee – Season Two, Volume 5
00313540 P/V/G..........................$16.99

Glee – Season Two, Volume 6
00313582 P/V/G..........................$16.99

Glee – Piano Play-Along Vol. 102
00312043 P/V/G..........................$14.99

Electronic Keyboard

Glee – E-Z Play Today Vol. 88
00100287................................$9.99

Piano

Glee
00316140 Easy Piano......................$14.99
00316148 Big-Note Piano..................$14.99
00316147 Five-Finger Piano...............$8.99

More Songs from Glee
00316150 Easy Piano......................$14.99

Glee – Easy Piano CD Play-Along Vol. 30
00312194 Book/CD Pack....................$14.99

Glee – The Christmas Album
00316162 Easy Piano......................$14.99

Glee – The Power of Madonna
00316142 Easy Piano......................$12.99

Glee – The Showstoppers
00316145 Easy Piano......................$14.99

Glee – Popular Songs Series
arr. Jennifer Linn
00296834................................$10.99

Glee – Piano Duet Play-Along Vol. 42
00290590 Book/CD Pack....................$16.99

Glee – The Warblers
00316169 Easy Piano......................$14.99

Glee – Season Two, Volume 4
00316158 Easy Piano......................$14.99

Glee – Season Two, Volume 5
00316159 Easy Piano......................$14.99

Glee – Season Two, Volume 6
00316173 Easy Piano......................$14.99

Guitar

Glee INCLUDES TAB
00702286 Easy Guitar – Notes & Tab...$16.99

Glee Guitar Collection INCLUDES TAB
00691050 Guitar Recorded Versions...$19.99

Vocal

Glee – The Singer's Series
00230061 Women's Edition Vol. 1........$14.99
00230062 Women's Edition Vol. 2........$14.99
00230063 Women's Edition Vol. 3........$14.99
00230064 Men's Edition Vols. 1-3.........$16.99
00230065 Duets Edition Vols. 1-3..........$16.99

Glee – Pro Vocal Book/CD Packs
00740437 Male/Female Edition Vol. 8...$15.99
00740440 Male/Female Edition Vol. 9...$19.99
00740443 Male/Female Edition Vol. 10...$14.99

Glee – Sing with the Choir Book/CD Pack
00333059 SATB.............................$16.99

Glee Vocal Method & Songbook
00312081 Book/CD Pack....................$14.99

FOR MORE INFORMATION, SEE YOUR LOCAL MUSIC DEALER,
OR WRITE TO:

HAL•LEONARD®
CORPORATION
7777 W. BLUEMOUND RD. P.O. BOX 13819 MILWAUKEE, WI 53213

Prices, contents and availability subject to change without notice.
www.halleonard.com

0811